Country Style
Soup & Sandwich

60 Delicious & Easy Recipes

Dianne Ireland

All rights reserved. No part of this publication may be reproduced, stored in a retrieval system or transmitted in any form or by any means- electronic, mechanical, photo copying, and recording of the author, except for brief passages quoted by a reviewer in a newspaper or magazine. To perform any of the above is an infringement of copyright law.

Disclaimer- This book is for enjoyment purposes only. I have prepared each and every one of these recipes and many of them countless times. Please read the instructions carefully before making. I cannot be responsible for any failures, loss or damage that may occur as a result of any recipe prepared.

With over whelming positive comments on my first cook book, Grandmama's Treasured Favorites & Traditional Recipes, I decided to publish inserts from this book with additional recipes for you to enjoy.

Thank you to a special lady, Carol VanSlyke, for reviewing and editing Country Style Soup & Sandwich.

ISBN-13: 978-1543069419
ISBN-10: 154306941X

Copyright 2017 - Dianne Ireland
Cover Design - Google
Printed by- Create Space in USA

E-mail: dfireso1@telus.net

In Memory
Mom & Dad

Thankful for my Mom and Dad's teachings. Many of these comfort foods were prepared in our kitchen on the farm.

My little kitchen
I love it's every nook
As I do my work
Wash pots and pans and cook
May the meals that I prepare
Be seasoned with love
And to those who enter my little kitchen
Enjoy these tasty meals.

INTRODUCTION

Although it's been almost four years since the release of my first cook book, it feels like yesterday.

When "GRANDMAMA'S TREASURED FAVORITES & TRADITIONAL RECIPES" came out in November 2013, I was unsure what the response would be. Originally it was my intension to create a book for my extended family. I envisioned a cookbook of favorite and traditional recipes taken from our family's past, while sharing stories and pieces of our family's history with our family members.

As I wrote my cookbook, I found that it was becoming a greater project and was emerging not only as a piece of family history but also historical information worthy of sharing with my larger community.

Unknown to me, there was a greater interest than I had expected. Bits and pieces of my stories and recipes became the starting point of animated reminiscing for others to share their own family traditions.

As a young girl, learning to prepare a meal was usually experimental with some successful and others not so successful. With determination and with a bit of creativity, I eventually learned how to cook by using whatever was in the cupboard. I collected recipes that looked interesting which I eventually made use of so that is why I always say, "be creative, try something new!"

Now, with another burst of energy and inspiration, I have written my second cook book, "COUNTRY STYLE SOUP & SANDWICH".

My aim is to share my enjoyment of creating and cooking by sharing a variety of ways to prepare a quick, easy and tasty sandwich which compliments a soup.

Whatever recipe you choose, a sandwich and a bowl of soup is a meal that appeals to anyone, anytime.

Remembering, a recipe is only a template to create your own fabulous sandwich by adding or deleting ingredients. Just experiment a little!

Today's sandwich is a masterpiece of your own delicious eatable creation. I encourage you to make use of the savory flavors of today in yesterday's sandwich.

I'd be delighted if you find that these tasty recipes regularly solve your lunch dilemmas. It is my hope that you will use these recipes to feed your family and even your friends from time to time.

ENJOY "COUNTRY STYLE SOUP & SANDWICH!"

CONTENTS

Introduction

Quick Soups
Page: 2-3

More Timely Soups
Page: 4-7

Sandwich Spreads
Page: 10

Cold Sandwiches
Page: 11-15

Hot Sandwiches
Page: 15-21

Dumplings & Noodles
Page: 24-25

Quick Breads & Buns
Page: 25-29

Pickles
Page: 30

Index
Pages: 31-34

SOUPS

Warming The Soul

What really is a soup?

SOUP is a liquid food with stock as its base and often containing pieces of solid food.

SO, soup should be something simple and delicious, adding your creation of savory spices and everything scrumptious. Soups are an experimental dish of fresh ingredients or left-overs from last night's dinner. Add spices to taste and maybe a few extra vegetables and possibly some meat to make the perfect soup. Or try adding a small amount of rice or macaroni or spaghetti or homemade noodles or maybe dumplings making an extra yummy soup. Soups can be frozen which is a real time saver.

Just holler soups on!

Little Bit Of Humor

*One time I was at a restaurant sitting at the next table to a customer who had ordered soup. When the waitress brought the soup to him, he stirred the soup and remarked, "Where are the vegetables?" She answered with a smile "go fishing," and walked away. Everyone chuckled.

*A fella invited his neighbor for lunch, as they walked into the house, he hollers, "Ma, add more water to the soup, we have company".

Tomato Macaroni Soup

2 cups water
1 can tomato soup
¼ cup onion – chopped fine
¼ cup celery – chopped fine
Salt, pepper, celery salt, onion salt - season to taste
1/8 cup macaroni – elbow or shell (small)

Fill saucepan with water and bring to a boil. Add onion and celery. Cook until tender; add macaroni continue to cook. Pour in tomato soup then add seasonings to taste, continue to cook on medium heat for about a ½ hour. Add more seasoning if required.

Vegetable Soup

2 cups water
1 can tomato soup
1 can vegetable broth
1 small onion - diced
2 sticks celery – diced - optional
4 carrots – diced
1 large potato diced
Salt & pepper
Onion salt or powder or dried flakes
Celery salt
Parsley flakes- dried or fresh

Fill saucepan with water and bring to a boil, add vegetables, cook until tender; add tomato soup and broth. Stir and add seasonings to taste. Cook on medium heat for about a ½ hour. Add more seasoning if required. Double recipe for extra servings.

Bean Wiener Soup
A quick and easy soup for anytime

2 cups water
1 can tomato soup
1 can pork/beans
½ small onion - chopped
3 sticks celery- chopped - optional
Salt & pepper – season to taste
4 wieners – cut into bite size
1/8 cup macaroni – optional

Fill medium saucepan with water and bring to a boil. Add onion, celery and macaroni, cook until tender; add tomato soup, pork/beans, pepper, salt, wieners. Stir well; continue to cook on medium heat for about a ½ hour. Add more seasoning if required.

Vegetable Rice Soup

2 cups water
1 can tomato soup
1 can vegetable broth
1 small onion - diced
2 sticks celery – diced - optional
4 carrots – diced
¼ cup rice – any kind
Salt & pepper
Onion salt or powder or dried flakes
Celery salt
Parsley flakes- dried or fresh

Fill saucepan with water and bring to a boil. Add vegetables and rice, cook vegetables until tender and rice is soft. Add tomato soup and broth. Stir, add seasonings to taste. Cook on medium heat for about a ½ hour. Add more seasoning if required. Double recipe for extra serving.

Dianne's Cabbage Soup

4 cups water
1 large onion - diced
2 cans of green cut beans or fresh beans - optional
2 large cans of whole tomatoes or stewed seasoned tomatoes
1 medium head of cabbage – chopped
6 sticks of celery – chopped
2 pkgs. onion soup mix or chicken noodle mix
2 lbs. of carrots – chopped
1 large can of beef or chicken broth
¼ tsp. salt, pepper, paprika, parsley.
Dash of Worcestershire sauce

Bring water to a boil. Cut onion, cabbage, carrots, celery into small pieces and add to boiling water. Stir, add remaining ingredients and seasonings. Cook for about 15 minutes then reduce heat to simmer, continue cooking till veggies are tender. May add more seasoning for taste. Makes a large pot

Beef Stew

5 cups water
1 lb. beef – cut into cubes
2 tbsps. olive oil – or other types of oils
2 large onions – diced
4 cups carrots – sliced
2 large potatoes – cut into cubes
2 cups turnips – cut into cubes
4 sticks of celery – diced – optional
Salt & pepper – season to taste
2 cubes of Beef Oxo

In a large nonstick pot, heat oil over medium to high heat. Add beef chunks; sauté until browned. Add onions; continue to sauté, stirring continuously until onions are clear in color. Add salt, pepper and Beef Oxo. Add water enough to cover the meat and onions. Bring to a boil then reduce heat to simmer until the meat is cooked and tender. May need to add more water and continue simmering. Add carrots, potatoes, celery, turnips and cover to continue to simmer until vegetables are tender. Simmering time about 1 hour (if the liquid is not covering the meat and vegetables add more water). Can add dumplings if desired

Turkey Noodle Soup

6 cups water
Turkey bones with meat on (roasted turkey leftovers)
2 cubes of chicken bouillon
1 cup cooked turkey – cubes
1 medium onion - diced
3 sticks celery – diced
4 carrots – diced
2 large potatoes diced
Salt & pepper
¼ tsp. onion salt or powder or dried flakes
¼ tsp. celery salt
¼ tsp. parsley flakes – dried or fresh
1 ½ cups egg noodles- dry or home made

Fill large pot with water, bring to a boil. Add cooked turkey bones with small amounts of meat on. Cook until meat falls off the bones. Remove bones, stir, and add chicken bouillon and seasonings to taste. Add cubed cooked turkey, onion, celery, carrots and potatoes and continue to cook until vegetables are tender; stir in noodles, continue to cook on medium heat for about a ½ hour or until noodles are soft and cooked. Add more seasoning if required.

French Onion Soup

2 tbsps. margarine
4 medium onions -sliced
4 cups beef stock or bouillon cubes
1 tsp. salt
1/8 tsp. black pepper
½ tsp. Worcestershire sauce
6 slices of bread – French
Parmesan cheese – grated
Croutons – optional

Melt margarine in frying pan. Slice onions diagonally, add to melted margarine, and cook gently until lightly browned, stir frequently. Spoon browned onions into a large sauce pan. Stir in beef stock, salt, pepper and Worcestershire sauce. Cover and simmer on medium heat for 30 minutes. Season to taste. Pour onion soup into bowls; add croutons (not too many) grate cheese over hot of soup. Can serve with toasted sliced bread on the side. Serves 6. Can be frozen

Old Country Borsch

2 to 3 lbs. beef soup bones
8 cups cold water
2 onions – sliced
2 stalks celery – cut into chunks
4 medium beets – peeled, sliced – make 2 cups
4 carrots – sliced thinly – make 1 ½ cups
1 small head cabbage – cut into chunks
½ green pepper – diced – optional
2 potatoes – cubed
1 tsp. salt
2 beets – coarsely grated – 1 cup
1 bay leaf
1 – 6oz. tomato paste
2 tbsps. vinegar
1 tbsp. sugar
2 tbsps. salt
8 oz. sour cream

In a large pot, cover bones with water and bring to boil. Skim foam off top of water, then simmer for 1 ½ to 2 hours or until meat falls off bones. Remove bones and cut meat into chunks. Set aside. Add onions, celery, beets carrots, cabbage, potatoes, green pepper, salt and bay leaf to boiling stock. Cover and cook about 30 minutes or until vegetables are tender. Add grated beets, tomato paste, vinegar, sugar, salt and meat. Simmer. Cover pot with a lid for 10 minutes. Just before serving add sour cream (do not boil) or wait till serving time, spoon sour cream on top of soup once in soup bowl. Makes 8 to 10 servings. Can be frozen.

Ham & Bean Soup

4 cups water
1 can tomato soup or diced canned tomatoes
1 can pork/beans
½ onion - chopped
3 sticks celery – chopped – optional
4 carrots - diced
2 potatoes- cubed
Salt & pepper – season to taste
1 cup cooked ham – leftover baked ham - cubed
Dumplings – optional

Fill medium saucepan with water and bring to a boil. Add onion, carrots, potatoes and celery. Cook until tender; add tomato soup, pork/beans, pepper, salt and ham. Stir well, and continue to cook on medium heat for about a ½ hour. Add more seasoning if required. Can add dumplings if desired.
Soups Ready!

SANDWICHES

EATABLE CREATIONS

To those who love making a great sandwich with your own added ingredients:

Try omitting margarine and use Miracle Whip or Mayonnaise (your choice) or mustard.

With a bit of a twist, mix mustard and Mayonnaise or Miracle Whip together to enhance the flavour.

To the ketchup lovers, try slathering ketchup on your toast and enjoy.

Perhaps omitting meat from a sandwich, making a veggie sandwich of any type of vegetable you want to eat.

Adding cheese or cheese whiz on a sandwich can also enhance the flavour.

Making a happy sandwich that will compliment your delicious soup.

Anything is possible, enjoy your creations!

Deviled Meat Spread

1 cup meat - chopped finely - wieners or canned meats or spreads or leftover cooked meats
1 dill pickle - chopped
2 tbsps. Miracle Whip

Mix all ingredients together until well mixed.
Spread on bread – various types or toast or halves of buns or crackers
Quick and easy, ready to serve for lunch.

Meat Spread

1 cup meat - chopped finely - wieners or canned meats or spreads or leftover cooked meats
¼ cup of onion -finely chopped
2 tbsps. Miracle Whip

Mix all ingredients together until well mixed. Spread on bread – various types or toast or halves of buns or crackers Great way to make a new creation

Salmon or Tuna Spreads

1 can salmon or tuna
¼ cup onion – Spanish or green chopped finely
½ cup Miracle Whip
Salt & pepper – season to taste

Mix all ingredients together until well mixed. Spread on bread – various types or buns or crackers. Quick and easy, ready to serve for lunch or afternoon tea.

Egg Salad Spread

2 eggs – boiled
Salt & pepper – season to taste
2 tbsps. Miracle Whip
1 green onion – chopped

Mix all ingredients together until well mixed. Ready to spread on a bun, crackers toast or bread.

Alternative Open Face Bun

1 bun – sliced in half
Egg or meat spread
Lettuce – enough to cover half of a bun or slice of bread
1 tsp. margarine
Salt & pepper - season to taste
Paprika – sprinkle – optional

Can toast bun or not, using any type of buns, spread margarine on bun, add lettuce then add egg or meat spread. Sprinkle with paprika, ready to serve. Serving for one.

Toasted Bacon Tomato Cheese & Lettuce Stacker

2 bread slices
1 cheese slice
3 bacon strips – cooked (pork or turkey)
½ tomato- sliced
Lettuce – enough to cover slice of bread
1 tsp. margarine
1 tbsp. Miracle Whip

Toast bread using any type of bread, spread margarine and Miracle Whip on toasted bread, add slice of cheese, tomato, lettuce and then add 3 strips of cooked bacon. Cover with second slice of bread. Cut in half and serve. KETCHUP PLEASE!

Red Onion Crisp Sandwich

2 slices of bread
5 onion slices - thinly cut
1 tsp. margarine
1 tbsp. Miracle Whip
1 slice of cheese - optional
Sprinkle of salt

Bread may be plain or toasted. Spread margarine and Miracle Whip onto bread, and then place sliced onion on top with a sprinkle of salt. Place second slice of bread on top and cut in half and ready to serve.

Garden Radish Sandwich

2 slices of bread
Radishes- sliced thinly
1 tsp. margarine
1 tsp. mayonnaise
Sprinkle of salt

Spread margarine onto both slices of bread, and then spread mayonnaise on one slice. Place sliced radishes onto mayonnaise, sprinkle with salt. Cover with second slice and cut in half, ready to serve. Serving for one.

Dill Pickle Sandwich

2 slices of bread
Dill pickles - sliced thinly
1 tsp. margarine

Spread margarine into both slices of bread, place sliced dill pickles on top of one slice of bread and cover with the other. Cut and ready to eat.

Elvis Banana & Peanut Butter Open Face Sandwich

1 slice of bread
1 banana - sliced
2 tbsps. peanut butter
1 tsp. margarine

Bread may be plain or toasted. Spread margarine and then the peanut butter onto bread, place sliced banana on top. Ready to eat. Serving for one

Old Cheddar & Syrup Sandwich

2 slices of bread
3 slices of old cheddar cheese
1 tsp. margarine
1 tbsp. syrup - Rodgers

Spread margarine onto both slices of bread, place sliced cheese on one slice. Spread on syrup. Cover with second slice of bread. Cut in half and serve.

Cinnamon Toast

1 slice of bread
1 tsp. margarine
Sugar
Cinnamon

Spread margarine on toasted bread, sprinkle sugar then cinnamon onto toast. Makes a great snack!

Peanut Butter & Jam Delites

2 slices of bread - any kind and can be toasted
Margarine
Peanut butter
Jam – any kind

Spread margarine on both slices of bread or toast. Add peanut butter on one slice then add jam over the peanut butter mixing together. Add second slice of bread or toast on top of the mixture. Cut in half and serve.

Fresh Lettuce Leaf Roll

1 large lettuce leaf
Sugar

Wash one large lettuce leaf, sprinkle with sugar, fold ends in and roll the leaf.

Turkey with Cranberry Sauce Sandwich

2 slices of bread - any kind
Cooked turkey - leftover roasted turkey
Margarine
Cranberry sauce - canned or cooked fresh cranberries

Spread margarine on both slices of bread. Place cold cooked turkey sliced or chunks onto one side of one slice of bread. Add cranberry sauce. Place second slice of bread on top and cut in half. Enjoy.

Chicken Salad Sandwich

2 slices of bread or bun - any kind and can be toasted
Margarine
Cooked chicken - leftovers from roasted chicken
1/8 of medium onion – finely chopped
1 tsp. Miracle Whip
Salt & pepper – season to taste

Mixture-
Cut cooked chicken into small pieces, add chopped onion and mix in a small bowl. Add Miracle Whip to the mixture and stir, Add spices. Mix again. Spread mixture onto one slice of buttered bread or bun or toast. Place second slice onto mixture and cut in half.
Serve with a pickle on the side.

Hamburger Bun

2 slices of bread or bun
Hamburger - left-over cooked patty or meat loaf (cold or hot)
Margarine
Hot mustard
Miracle Whip
Lettuce
Tomato
Cheese - slice or cheese whiz

Spread margarine onto both slices of bread or bun. Then spread hot mustard and Miracle Whip onto one slice of bread or bun. Add leaf of lettuce, slice of tomato and cheese. Add a cooked hamburger patty or slice of meat loaf. Place second slice on top and cut in half. Can serve with a dab of ketchup and a sliced pickle or tomato on the side.

Simple Cheese Pepperoni Bunwich

1 cheese bun
1 pepperoni stick
Margarine

Slice open cheese bun, spread margarine on and then add pepperoni stick. Fold and ready to eat.

Sardine Finest

1 tin sardines
2 slices of bread or bun or crackers
Margarine
Lettuce - optional
Miracle Whip
Salt & pepper - season to taste

Spread margarine onto both slices of bread or bun. In a small bowl mix sardines, Miracle Whip, salt and pepper together. Spread onto one slice of bread or bun. (can spread on crackers) Add leaf of lettuce if desired. Place second slice on top and cut in half.

Veggie Wrap

1 wrap - any type
Lettuce - shredded or leaf
1 tomato slice - thinly sliced
¼ small carrot - grated
½ tsp. ranch or cucumber dressing
1 onion slice - optional
Salt & pepper –season to taste
Cream cheese or any type of cheese – optional
Cucumber - optional

Lay wrap flat, spread dressing or cream cheese; add lettuce, tomato, carrot, cucumber or onion. Sprinkle with salt and pepper. Fold ends in and roll the wrap.

Grilled Apple & Goat Cheese Sandwich

2 slices bread or 1 flatbread
1 apple - sliced
1 tbsp. goat cheese -raspberry or plain
Margarine

Spread cheese onto bread or flatbread. Lay sliced apple on cheese. Spread margarine on outside of bread or flatbread. Place on hot grill cook until golden brown.

Grilled Cheese & Ham Panini

1 Panini
Cheese - cheddar or mozzarella
Slice of ham
Margarine

Heat grill. Place cheese and ham on Panini. Fold. Spread margarine on outside of both sides of Panini. Place on hot grill and cook until golden brown OR heat an oiled frying pan and grill Panini until golden brown on one side then flip over and cook until golden brown.

Make Your Own Pizza Bun

3 buns – plain or onion
1 – 7 ½ oz. can tomato sauce or tomato soup
¼ tsp. oregano
½ tsp. garlic salt- optional
½ tsp. lemon pepper-optional
8 oz. cheddar cheese – medium or mozzarella – grated

In a small bowl mix tomato soup and spices together. Spread generously on a plain or onion bun halves. Arrange toppings of choice on top. Sprinkle cheese over topping. Place in an oven and broil until top bubbles.
Serves 6

Suggested Toppings-

Olives - finely chopped
Salami, pepperoni, ham - diced or sliced
Mushrooms - fresh sliced or canned pieces
Green Peppers - sliced
Onion - sliced thinly
Pineapple – chunks or crushed (drained)

Hot Ham Cheese & Egg Sandwich

2 bread slices
1 cheese slice
1 ham slice- cooked
1 egg - fried
1 tsp. margarine

Toast bread using any type of bread, spread margarine on toasted bread, add slice of ham and cheese, and then add one fried egg. Cover with second slice of bread and cut in half, ready to serve.
Oh YOU MAY NEED KETCHUP!

English Muffin Bacon Egger

1 English Muffin
Margarine
1 bacon slice
1 egg
Salt & pepper   to season
Cheese - optional

Toast English Muffin, and then spread margarine on. Cook bacon, and then cook egg in a frying pan. Place bacon and egg onto one half of muffin, add cheese, and cover with other half of muffin. Serve with a dab of ketchup.

Meat & Cheese Sandwich

2 bread slices
1 cheese slice
1 meat slice - any type of cooked meat –beef, ham, chicken
1 tsp. margarine
1 tsp. mustard
Lettuce - optional
Tomato - optional

Plain or toasted bread using any type of bread, spread margarine and mustard on bread, add slice of cheese and then meat. Place second slice of bread on top. Cut in half and ready to serve.

Grilled Cheese Sandwich

2 slices of bread
1 cheddar cheese - slice
1 tsp. margarine
1 tbsp. oil
Meat slices- optional
Onion slices - thinly cut

Take two slices of bread, place sliced cheese and (onion if using), and in between two slices of bread, then spread margarine on the outsides of the two slices. Prepare by heating skillet on medium heat, add oil then place sandwich into the skillet. Once one side is golden brown, turn over and brown the other side. Ready to serve hot.

Toasted Fried Egg & Cheese Sandwich

2 slices of bread
1 cheddar cheese - slice
1 egg - fried
1 tsp. margarine
1 tbsp. oil
Salt & pepper to season

Toast bread using any type of bread, spread margarine on toasted bread, add slice of cheese and fried egg. Add salt and pepper to season. Slice in half and ready to serve.

Country Toasted Fried Egg Sandwich

2 slices of bread
1 egg - fried
1 tsp. margarine
Salt & pepper to season

Toast bread using any type of bread, spread margarine on toasted bread, and add fried egg. Add salt and pepper to season. Cut in half and ready to serve. Serving for one

Open Face Cheese Toast

1 slice of bread
Cheese - cheddar or mozzarella
1 tsp. margarine

Toast bread, spread margarine on toast and place sliced hard cheese on top. Place toast into boiler oven and cook until cheese is melted. Serving for one. Can omit margarine

Campfire Toasted Cheese Sandwich

2 slices of bread
Cheese Whiz or cheddar
1 tbsp. margarine
Foil wrap

Spread cheese between two slices of bread, spread margarine on the outside of the two sides. Wrap into foil wrap with shinny side inward. Place foiled sandwich on a stick or a barbeque fork and hold over an open fire, turning occasionally until done. Now it's time for a campfire grilled cheese sandwich. Great on a snowmobile outings or camping!

Easy Weiner Wrap

8 wieners
Pillsbury dough
Cheese slices

Open container; roll out dough, cutting along the perforated lines. Place one wiener and one slice of cheese on a triangle of dough, roll starting at an angle. Repeat until all 8 wieners are used. Place onto a greased baking sheet. Bake at 350F. for 15 to 20 minutes or until golden brown. Turn each wrap over once, to ensure both sides are golden brown.

Special Fried Bologna Toast

2 slices of bread
1 tbsp. margarine
Hot mustard
Cheese slice -optional
Oil

Slice bologna about ½ inch thickness, place in an oil heated frying pan. Fry until golden brown on both sides. Toast bread, spread margarine and mustard onto the toasted bread; place a slice of warm fried bologna between two slices of toasted bread. Can add slice of cheese or pickles, cut in half and serve.

Country Style Hot Ham & Cheese Sandwich

2 slices of bread
1 egg-beaten
¾ cup milk
Cheese - any type
Ham - slice if desired
¼ tsp. salt

Spread margarine lightly on bread. On one slice arrange a slice of ham and a thin slice of cheese and put another slice of bread on top. In a medium bowl mix milk, beaten egg and salt together. Dip both sides of sandwich into egg mixture. Place dipped egg sandwich in an oil heated frying pan and cook. Turning over once, cooking until both sides are lightly golden brown. Serve hot.

Frankfurter & Sauerkraut Dog

1 frankfurter or hot dog bun or any type of bun
1 frankfurter or sausage
1 tbsp. margarine
Mustard -any type
¼ cup sauerkraut - pre-cooked

Grill a frankfurter or sausage. Spread margarine and mustard on an open bun. Add pre-cooked cold sauerkraut onto the bun. Add cooked hot sausage. Fold and enjoy.

County Style Scramble Egg & Bacon Sandwich

2 slices of bread - any type and can be toasted
1 egg - beaten
1 slice bacon - cooked and diced
Margarine
1/8 onion - chopped - optional
Salt & pepper

Heat frying pan; add bacon and onion, stir occasionally until cooked. In a small bowl add egg, salt and pepper, beat mixture. Pour egg mixture over bacon and onion, stir until cooked. Place egg mixture onto a buttered slice of bread or toast. Place second slice on top of egg mixture. Cut in half and serve with Ketchup on the side.

Barbequed Pulled Pork Bun

1 bun -any type
Cooked hot pulled pork
Margarine -optional

Spread margarine on both sides of bun. Spoon hot pulled pork onto half of bun, fold and ready to eat. Can be served with coleslaw as a side dish.

Taco Filling

1 lb. ground hamburger
1 can tomato soup
Oil
Salt & pepper
1/8 onion - chopped
1 tsp. chili spice – season to taste

Heat oiled skillet pan, add onions. Cook until done then add hamburger. Continue to cook until well done. Stir constantly. Add tomato soup, salt, pepper and chili spice. Stir; continue to cook for about five minutes. Add more chili spice if desired. Ready to serve on homemade Fried Bread or Taco shells.

COMPLIMENTS

TO
SOUPS

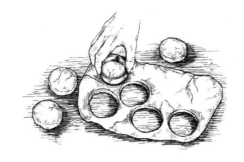

Baking with love
Provides food
For the soul

Plain Dumplings

2 cups flour
1 tbsp. baking powder
½ tsp. salt
¼ tsp. pepper
1 tsp. parsley flakes - fresh or dried
1 cup milk

In medium bowl mix flour, baking powder, salt, pepper, and parsley flakes together. Add milk gradually pouring in half a cup at a time, mixing thoroughly. Continue to add liquid until the dough is completely mixed and sticky. When soup or stew is cooked, add one tablespoon of dough at a time on top of the soup or stew. Allow space from the top of the pot to let the dumplings rise. Cover with a lid and continue to cook on medium heat. Turn dumplings over once and continue to cook until the dumplings are fluffy and not sticky inside.

Dumplings

I cup flour
1 tbsp. baking powder
½ tsp. salt
½ cup water
2 tsps. oil

In a small bowl mix flour, baking powder and salt together. In a separate bowl combine water and oil together, mixing slightly. Gradually pour liquid into dry ingredients until dough is completely mixed and sticky. Drop teaspoons of dumpling dough on top of hot soup or stew, cover and continue to cook on medium heat. Allow to simmer, cooking for 12 to 15 minutes.

Homemade Noodles

3 egg yolks
1 whole egg
3 tsps. cold water
1 tsp. salt
2 cups flour

In a medium size bowl beat egg yolks and whole egg together; add water and continue to beat mixture, add salt and stir. Add flour gradually mixing in until the dough is stiff. Kneading the dough mixture until dough is soft but not sticky. On a floured surface, roll the dough thinly to about 1/8 inches thick. Cut into narrow strips 1/8 inch to ½ inch wide. Let the dough dry for about 10 minutes. Ready to drop into soup, one strip at a time. When cooked the noodles should be raised and soft.

Baked Bannock

5 ½ cups flour
3 ½ tbsps. baking powder
Pinch of salt
4 ½ tbsps. lard
3 cups flour - if needed
Water as required

In a large bowl mix 5 ½ cups of flour, baking powder and salt together. Add lard into dry mixture using a fork or pastry blender. Mix until ingredients are crumbly. Add small amounts of water slowly into mixture gently mixing with a fork. Mix until the mixture is thickened and dough is formed. On a floured surface, knead dough gently until soft (add small amounts of flour if too sticky) Do not overwork the dough. Shape and flatten with a rolling pin or by hand. Dough should be ½ inch thick. Cut bannock with cookie cutter or any kitchen tool (drinking glass or cup). Grease cookie sheet. Bake 350 degrees F for 15 minutes to 20 minutes until golden brown (checking every 4 minutes). Makes about 10 pieces – depending on size. Also dough can be placed in a greased 8" x 10" cake pan and baked for 25 minutes or until golden brown. Once cooked and cooled cut into squares.

Fried Bannock

3 cups flour
2 ½ tbsps. baking powder
Pinch of salt
3 ½ cups cold water
Lard

Mix dry ingredients together in a medium bowl. Add small amounts of water slowly, mixing gently with a fork until dough forms a ball. Then knead dough gently forming a soft ball and not sticky. On floured surface flatten dough with a rolling pin or by hand. Dough should be about ½ inch thick. Cut dough into small pieces and then shape onto circles. Melt enough lard in a pan for deep frying. Heat until hot. Place one piece at a time into the hot grease, cooking about 2 minutes, turning frequently to make sure the bannock is cooked evenly and light brown. Serve warm. Will make about 14 pieces depending on size of each piece.

Fry Bread

1 ½ cups flour
1 tsp. baking powder
1 tbsp. margarine - melted
½ cup warm milk
Pinch of salt
4 tbsps. oil

Mix dry ingredients together, stir in melted margarine and milk until well mixed. On a floured surface knead dough until smooth. Divide into four pieces. Shape each piece into flat circles. Heat oil in frying pan on medium heat. Fry dough rounds one at a time until lightly brown on both sides. Makes 4 pieces. Can be eaten plain or make Indian Tacos. Just add taco filling on top and fold.

Beaver Tails

½ cup warm water
5 tsps. yeast - dry
1 pinch sugar
1/3 cup warm milk
1/3 cup sugar
1 ½ tsps. salt
1 tsp. vanilla
2 eggs - beaten
1/3 cup oil
5 cups flour - may not need all 5 cups
Vegetable oil - for frying
2 tbsps. of cinnamon and 1 cup white sugar – for mixture coating

In a large bowl place warm water, yeast, and pinch of sugar. Allow to stand a couple minutes until yeast swells and dissolves. Stir gently. Add in sugar, warm milk, vanilla, beaten eggs, oil, and salt. Stir. Add flour, one cup at a time until dough is soft and not sticky. Knead dough for 5 to 8 minutes until dough is smooth and elastic. Place in a greased bowl. Cover with cloth. (Place bowl of dough into a plastic bag and seal if not using right away). Let rise for 30 to 40 minutes. Gently poke to deflate. Pinch off golf ball size pieces of dough. On a lightly floured surface roll each ball shape into oval shapes using a rolling pin. Cover with cloth while preparing to heat oil in a pan. Heat about 2 inches of oil in fryer or in pan. Stretch each dough piece into a beaver tail shape. Drop dough into heated oil. One to two pieces at a time. Turn dough over once to fry until golden brown. Cool. Mix cinnamon and sugar together. Dip each fried beaver tail into sugar cinnamon mixture. Ready to enjoy

Quick Drop Biscuits

1 ¾ cups flour
½ tsp. salt
3 tsps. baking powder
6 tbsps. margarine
1 cup milk
½ cup cheese - grated - optional

Preheat oven to 450 degrees F. Mix together flour, salt, and baking powder in a medium bowl. Add margarine, mixing into dry ingredients until well blended to a crumbly mixture. Add grated cheese if desired. Add milk and mix until crumbly mixture turns into thick dough. Do not over mix. The dough should be sticky. Grease muffin tin. Drop dough into each cup filling half full. Bake for 12 to 15 minutes. Biscuits should be slightly golden brown.

Baking Powder Biscuits

1 ¾ cups flour
2 tbsps. sugar
1 tbsp. baking powder
3 tbsps. margarine
¾ cup milk

Preheat oven to 450 degrees F. Grease a baking sheet with oil. Set aside. In a large bowl, mix together flour, sugar and baking powder. Using a fork or pastry blender, cut the margarine into the flour mixture until coarse crumbs form. Quickly stir in milk until soft dough is formed. On a lightly floured surface, with a rolling pin or by hand roll dough to a ½ inch thickness. Using a 2 ½ inch biscuit cutter (drinking glass or cup) cut out biscuits. Gather trimmings into a ball then flatten, re-roll, and cut out more biscuits until all the dough is used. Place biscuits on prepared baking sheet. Bake until golden brown, about 12 to 15 minutes. Place biscuits on a wire rack to cool. Can be frozen.

Cheese Biscuits

1 cup flour
3 tsps. baking powder
¼ tsp. salt
1 tsp. margarine
½ cup cheddar cheese - grated
½ cup milk

Mix flour, baking powder and salt together, add margarine and grated cheese, using a fork blending together until crumbly. Add milk and stir until ingredients are well mixed. On a slightly floured surface, roll out the dough to a ½ inch thickness. Using a 2 ½ inch biscuit cutter (drinking glass or cup) cut out each biscuit. Gather trimmings into a ball then flatten, re-roll, and cut out more biscuits until all the dough is used. Place biscuits on greased baking sheet. Bake at 450 degrees F. until golden brown, about 12 to 15 minutes. Place biscuits on a wire rack to cool. Can be frozen.

2 Hour Buns

3 cups lukewarm water
8 tbsps. sugar
6 tsps. oil
1 tsp. salt
2 tbsps. yeast - fast rising
2 eggs
7 - 8 cups flour or enough to make workable dough.

In a large bowl beat eggs one at a time. Add sugar, salt, oil and water. Whip until well mixed. Add yeast and sugar, letting yeast dissolve then gently stir. Add flour until soft dough forms. Knead dough, adding small amounts of flour until not sticky. Let rise for 15 minutes, punch down gently and let rise again for another 15 minutes. Form dough into buns. Grease baking pan, place buns on baking pan, let buns rise to double, and then bake at 350 degrees F. for 25 minutes or until golden brown. Can be frozen.

Refrigerator Pickles

Brine-
4 cups white sugar
4 cups vinegar
1 ¾ tsps. celery seed
1 1/3 tsps. mustard seed
1 ½ tsps. turmeric
1/3 cup pickling salt

In canner or large pot add sugar, vinegar and spices together, bring to a boil, stirring until sugar and pickling salt is dissolved.

Cucumber Mixture-
12 cups cucumbers - thinly sliced
3 to 6 cups small white onions - peeled
1 medium size cauliflower - cut into bite size pieces – optional

Add cucumbers, onions and cauliflower to hot brine and stir. Let sit in canner or large pot cooling for 24 hours. Place pickles in a medium size (ice cream) plastic pail or sterilized jars, making sure the brine cover the pickle mixture. Cover with lid and place in the fridge. Will keep for several months.
Compliments a great sandwich!

INDEX
Pages

QUICK SOUPS

Tomato Macaroni Soup -2

Vegetable Soup -2

Bean Wiener Soup -3

Vegetable Rice Soup -3

MORE TIMELY SOUPS

Dianne's Cabbage Soup -4

Beef Stew -4

Turkey Noodle Soup -5

French Onion Soup -5

Old Country Borsch -6

Ham & Bean Soup -7

SANDWICH SPREADS

Deviled Meat Spread -10

Meat Spread -10

Salmon or Tuna Spreads -10

Egg Salad Spread -10

INDEX
Pages

Continue....

<u>COLD SANDWISHES</u>

Alternate Open Face Bun -11

Toasted Bacon Tomato Cheese & Lettuce Stacker -11

Red Onion Crisp Sandwich -11

Garden Radish Sandwich -12

Dill Pickle Sandwich -12

Elvis Banana & Peanut Butter Open Face Sandwich -12

Old Cheddar & Syrup Sandwich -12

Cinnamon Toast -13

Peanut Butter & Jam Delites -13

Fresh Lettuce Leaf Roll -13

Turkey with Cranberry Sauce Sandwich -13

Chicken Salad Sandwich -14

Hamburger Bun -14

Simple Cheese Pepperoni Bunwich -14

Sardine Finest -15

Veggie Wrap -15

INDEX
Pages

Continue....

<u>HOT SANDWICHES</u>

Grilled Apple & Goat Cheese Sandwich -15

Grilled Cheese & Ham Panini -16

Make Your Own Pizza Bun -16

Hot Ham Cheese & Egg Sandwich -17

English Muffin Bacon Egger -17

Meat & Cheese Sandwich -17

Grilled Cheese Sandwich -18

Toasted Fried Egg & Cheese Sandwich -18

Country Toasted Fried Egg Sandwich -18

Open Face Cheese Toast -19

Campfire Toasted Cheese Sandwich -19

Easy Weiner Wrap -19

Fried Bologna Special Toast -20

County Style Hot Ham & Cheese Sandwich -20

Frankfurter & Sauerkraut Dog -20

Country Style Scramble Bacon & Egg Sandwich -21

Barbequed Pulled Pork Bun -21

Taco Filling -21

INDEX
Pages

Continue....

COMPLIMENTS TO SOUPS

Plain Dumplings -24

Dumplings -24

Homemade Noodles -25

Baked Bannock -25

Fried Bannock -26

Fry Bread -26

Beaver Tails -27

Quick Drop Biscuits -28

Baking Powder Biscuits -28

Cheese Biscuits -29

2 Hour Buns -29

COMPLIMENTS TO SANDWICHES

Refrigerator Pickles -30

ABOUT THE AUTHOR

Dianne Ireland grew up in a Northern Alberta farming community. She is the author of Grandmama's Treasured Favorites & Traditional Recipes and My Battle & Beyond – Silent Journey Living with Sarcoidosis. Dianne recently retired, now resides in Peace River, Alberta.

Recipes/Notes
****

Recipes/Notes
****

Made in the USA
Columbia, SC
19 April 2017